Persistence of Perception

poems by

Nathan J. Reid

Finishing Line Press
Georgetown, Kentucky

Persistence of Perception

Publisher: Leah Maines

Editor: Christen Kincaid

Cover Art and Design: Alaina Albaugh

Author Photo: Ashley E Beranek

Printed in the USA on acid-free paper.
Order online: www.finishinglinepress.com
also available on amazon.com

Author inquiries and mail orders:
Finishing Line Press
P. O. Box 1626
Georgetown, Kentucky 40324
U. S. A.

TABLE OF CONTENTS

TRAVELING CHARACTER ACTORS

HINDSIGHT & OTHER VISIONS

KALACHAKRA (PART 2)

To Blake Cadkin,
whom I wish to drink coffee with again someday
in the Restaurant at the End of the Universe.

Moritūrī tē salūtāmus.

Say It Live

In the shower I write poetry.
My fingers drip cursive words across the tiles that lift off
like skinless water balloons, drift around my home.
I stick my head in them several times a day, get my scalp wet,
                        meditate.
            I write poems
with crushed soda cans on their tires and trading cards in their spokes
poems that play Ghost in the Graveyard with sardines and the streetlight gang
they lick the Babel fish and try talking to Bigfoot.

    In blue jeans I write poetry.
I see souls and bits of souls staggered like backyard fences
they hunch over a rain barrel and quilt together days from all our echoes
some echoes are faint and fragile eggs about to break like reborn bone
        some echoes beat like a drum
as school kids we searched the grounds for so many dinosaur fossils
but tree roots and lost twigs were all we ever found, or at least
that is what some very clever fossils led us to believe.

    In pajamas I write poetry
where Little Miss Muffet sits on her tuffet gazing down upon Mordor
she cracks knuckles like black pepper, polishes her spoon, then devours
her midnight snack as she dreams in the pink and peaceful grass.

    In dreams I write poetry
with uninvented words and psychic sunshine
without burden of translation
I steer starships toward the dark matter of language
toward a theory of symbolism
        steer them toward…

KALACHAKRA
(PART 1)

Brahman: Reveries of Manvantara

a singing storyteller pleads everything
be his muse, be here, be mine
o crooked nothings and silent knuckles
sorry tomorrows crave sky after sky

an evershining sun dwells in dreams named Solstice & Winter

so see here, storyteller
be here the bend and see here, storyteller
you must let I be thine
must sing, plead

may a deeply rooted
bark-wrapped straw

suck all water
from underground wells

pull hydration
through countless canals

and feed those evergreen fireworks
frozen in explosion

Natural Blend 1

orange purple rays embrace wave-worn yellow sand
breathe the newborn air, how its warmth melts icy snow
while a glacier travels with ease Antarctica dreams that
hail hits a flower, destroys the petals waving, Mother Nature

kills and buries its kill in Mother Earth's coffee:

the fresh aroma of dirt: invigorating

the fresh aroma of dirt:

invigorating

Chipper the (Dead) Chipmunk

My roommate and I found Chipper in the fall of 2010
floating face-down in a green five-gallon bucket.

He must have climbed in searching for a mound of nuts or grains
and discovered instead that he couldn't swim, clasping
to autumn leaves that refused to carry him across the water.

We thought we might fish him out, kick the bucket over, let its contents cascade
down the concrete steps that led to the laundry room—but winter came, so we
let him stay, told friends about his arctic tomb within the circular brick of ice.
We wondered what he might look like by spring: frost-bitten, water-logged,
emptied of bodily gases. We kept saying to each other, *Okay,*

     but do you think he'll still float?

        …April came.

We grew giddy as ice thawed toward transparency, the rotten leaves
darkening, dampening, starting to move, the sun's rebirthing light
piercing its way through the tomb, until one day we came home
to see our landlord had cleaned—green bucket overturned, contents gone.

We stared at that hollow memorial for a full minute, maybe more.

Then went inside without a word, strangely missing him.

This Just In – Local Ant News Bulletin (Broadcast Date: June 5, 2010)

Ant hills around the nation are raising awareness of a new danger triggering an old familiar fear. After the Big Wheel Epidemic of '81, the Magnifying Glass Massacre of '93, and the more recent 2008 Water Balloon Bombings, ants everywhere are now bracing themselves against a new threat:

Incredibly fat human toddlers.

A fatal incident occurred last week when a small ant community living under the Northside Park swing set was entirely crushed as a child jumped onto a swing and snapped the chain. Officials have announced there are so far no survivors and it could take weeks to identify those individuals not wearing their lifting licenses at the time the tragedy took place. They are survived by a colony of red cousins living under the Northside slide, and their exoskeletons. Rallies involving picnic marches are on the rise and demonstrations on top of ice cream cones are being held all across the country as the Toddler Terror of 2010 ignites panic everywhere.

More at eleven.

Not Humid

This is not the drenching hum of humidity.
It is the soft roar of a cool-blue waterfall.

This is mist kissing peppermint to your forehead
sending blasts of brisk mountain brooks
from the tips of your fingernails to the pads of your toes.

This is you hiding inside a crisp shade, waxy fronds fanning your face
as silvery thoughts aerate in breezy circulation.

This is your skull—a pitcher of icy lemonade, a frothing root beer float—
a cold beverage, sweating.

This September

a fresh light conceived

the long road can't remember
what blind trees foretold

seek these hideaways:
>   soft hills singing old silos
>   spiced-leaf salted pumpkin seed
>   pond-prints & brainstreams
>   M&M-lit caramel apples, still warm

cumulo-green neon swells the sky
as electric pistils uncoil
plant wiry kisses on boom-petals

hazy raindrops bring shimmering renaissance
as if the true version of the ground were a wet one

Natural Blend 2

warmth melts icy snow, a glacier travels with ease, Antarctica dreams
of orange purple rays embracing wave-worn yellow sand
breathe the newborn air from Mother Earth's coffee
the fresh aroma of dirt invigorating all the cruel and beautiful
drowning and refreshing irreversible storms where hail
hits a flower, destroys the petals waving, Mother Nature kills

Mother Nature kills and yet a deeply rooted bark-wrapped straw
pulls hydration through countless canals, grows its flesh of green

Mother Nature kills and yet
                                    it is spring

Spring Makes True

Spring makes true the wild trails
we dreamt ambling all winter
where the weather smiles so brightly
we must step off the road to meet it
without soaked laces or muddy soles
where gravel is friendly, inspiring folk songs

Spring makes true the unlocked sun
where rainbows escape through prism bars
coating our skin with a simmering sense
we possessed formerly in hibernation
where not the bird, nor the song, nor the nest, nor the tree
but *the egg* is eyed as most beautiful

Spring makes true forgotten rain
rebirthing our spirits, thawing thoughts
over sunflowers, converting us from
adult to embryo to child to adult again
where warm nights keep windows yawning
as loose cloth giggles on toward summer

IN
THESE
WALLS

Spare Room

Welcome to the spare room, where good little trinkets go to die.
They wait in their boxes. Cold and mouthless.
Keeping our secrets from us but only for a while.

This is where love letters are lost deliberately, where random
jigsaw pieces pop into existence, where the unwanted gift is tossed.

This is where Christian families resurrect Christmas trees year after year like
mocking messiahs. This is where father and son each keeps his stash of porn,
unaware of the other's stash of course because that would be *very awkward*. It
would be even more awkward if they knew this is where mom hides her first-
ever vibrator, in a sock, in a shoebox, a shoebox that at a glance would appear
to only be filled with old make-up and *Oh my heavens, if the children ever found
it…*This is where a birthday-suited young man franticly hides his birthday-
suited girlfriend and shuts the door, for his family has come home sooner than
expected. This is where unpruned strings of personality are tied and tucked
away. This is where the office, the guest bed, music room, workout equipment,
extra TV, art studio, or personal library was going to go but I guess
         we never quite got around to it.

This is the spare room—the wild card of every home
                    waiting to discover you.

Some people know the space like their favorite jacket.
Some people see the room twice in its entirety: once when they move in,
once when they move out, and sometimes not even then.

Or maybe your spare room doesn't exist in any house.
Maybe it's the plastic tub you keep in storage
         the backpack on your shoulder
         the bottom of your purse
         the backseat of your car.

Or maybe it's a child's suitcase found in your parents' basement
filled with old friends you thought you'd never see again.

Wherever it is: Welcome to the spare room.
         It is waiting to discover you.

he asked:
how big is a thought inside my mind?

they replied:
the same size as a human inside the universe

Happy Dream

haven't felt like this
since I was four years old
sprawled out on my back
in summer grass
wearing bright blue overalls
arm blocking the sun
little body so light
I could fall into the sky

Sawdust Days

Eat chocolate soft serve in a cone.
Skip rocks against the waves.
Ride tiny trains with tiny people.
Get your walks in before this warm day burns away.

Love that gal in the summer green dress.
Love that guy in the blue shirt, the khaki shorts.
Grab that hand through cotton candy, the calliope.
Lock those kissing memories inside the season, buried in the sand,
    whispering on and on and on from shore.

Sunday Sacrifices

All these tiny ant carcasses sprinkle the sidewalk
like used-up matches on a barroom floor. Steady
must be my hands when focusing sunlight through
the magnifying glass, onto the concrete below, squatting
with perfect balance to prevent toppling over and dirtying
my Sunday best.

The licorice bits of life scurry toward the grass, vainly
attempt escape from the invisible flame as it zips across
their playing field, consuming their herd one by one.

Kept

I lose footraces, daydreamed lovers, daredevil bike rides,
cops & robbers, ninja turtles, marble rollers, sardines,
sticks for swords, the drooling aromas of folded pizza,
cocktail wieners, mashed potatoes igniting our school
cafeteria: a gymnasium that shrinks with time, with too many
sleepless nights at too young an age, clutching to 60s rock
lullabies while the room protects me against scary stories
come to life in naked darkness, hallucinations creeping toward me
between the shifting glows of passing cars, I whisper *demons*
beware! I roll in magic blankets, Batman underwear, and own a Nerf gun!
and the sheets and songs and worried old house keep me, spill me into
a morning softened by Grandma Reid's rendition of *Jeepers Creepers,*
by her pocketfuls of vitamin C drops, Lifesavers, sour ball candies that help
heal broken bones, crimson cuts, stairs that have no railings—the falls become
dried-up wounds, wrinkled scabs, and once-upon-a-times where band-aids
           could be the enemy

yes yes

haste makes waste
smudges hold grudges
practice makes better
and all that withers
is not old

AMP

       I awake before my alarm
the earthy pulse of nirvana still seeping from my dreams
a small yawn escapes, I unruffle my sheets, lift myself into a new cage
of petite pops and creaks that follows me down the hall

in the kitchen I smack two eggs together, catch toast as it flies past my plate
bacon hisses in its fat, the pan scrapes, my fork knits food into my mouth
I toss the dishes in the sink, go hop in the shower, where my shower caddy
holds bottles of different melodies for how to start my day, I click one open,
rub its hopeful tones through my hair: piano-cavern-ocean-silk lathering my
scalp, collecting in milky pearls that realize themselves, roll down my body,
clink against the bottom of the tub, the water is sweet and youthful

the fan buzzes, the knob squeaks, I dry dress brush my teeth
a brief flurry of shoelace, my alarm goes off—fingers stomp it out
I grab my keys, the door to the back porch gasps
I secure the lock, trot down the steps, start my car

a stick breaks as the seat belt slides into place, I roll down my window
wheels lick the road, engines huff, the birds are candied glass
wind holds up the branches and sunlight poking through is like synth in a
funk song, it tries to groove with me—but the rhythm is lost
        as a string of sirens go doppling by

I park in front of the coffee shop, slip inside into a cloud
of coughing-chewing-swallowing, of ceramic conversations
someone's crunching an apple, someone's stirring a beverage
there is not one but two crying babes, my head is slightly pounding
through a vortex of steam and foam I emerge with my drink, drive to work
fingernails scratching sandpaper stubble at every stoplight

the office is cold: keyboards and computer mice tap out
a pattering popcorn limbo upon which staplers, empty stomachs,
and electric pen scribbles dance for eight hours, until the janitor
          vacuums them away…

I'm riding again with the open window, there's a fly stuck in my ear
lines of vehicles thread back from the red flipping coins of a railroad crossing
I stop, drivers have started honking, the train is a few short seconds away

an old man sits, stalled at the tracks, stuck between panic and a seat belt
people yell, people wave, but the industrial beast charges at a man now slow
with age, whistling a contrast of color, its mission: to remind us that grey is not
one tune but a well-rounded musician—just as the old man frees himself,
opens his door to safety, the locomotive POUNCES, THE PEOPLE
SCREAM, METAL SHRIEKS ROARING LIKE A THOUSAND
SKINLESS NIGHTMARES GAPING OPEN HORROR LOVE-FEARED
CARRIES WRECKAGE INTO DARKNESS AS FIFTY PEOPLE BLINK
INTO A WORLD OF RECORD NEEDLE STATIC THAT CLIMBS TO
THE INSANE SUMMIT OF TINNITUS, NUMBING US, CARRYING
EACH OF US INTO DARKNESS, MY MIND WANDERS HOME BY
THE BEAT OF A FROZEN DRUM, I PARK AMONG A CHOIR OF
SIX-FOOT CICADAS, BUST INSIDE, CRASH THE STAIRS, RIP MYSELF
UP THROUGH MY BEDROOM DOOR AND SLAM THE STORM

OUT!

silence

the ghost of sound

dwelling in my breath, going round and round like a peaceful planet
bringing forth that sweet song I had forgotten in my dreams
unveiling that fragile humming light of a hologram we call soul

it releases me

an earthy pulse begins to play, my blanket is a star-kissed leaf

my blanket is a star-kissed leaf

as I sleep

Music Lovers

a single moment
       frozen in its own epiphany
new and unheard

we can't help but silence
       our selfish consciousness
       give our full attention
forget how our own hearts beat

ears long rusted shut
       now open
address everything else as hush

eternal fragments inhale our breath
       exist through us
       exist exactly for that purpose
then let us go before we're ready

before any of us realize what's been played
       and what can still be sung

In These Walls

I hollowed out a spoon, spoke through it to you, my voice broadcasting blips and static vinyl lips like an old Victrola, blowing heat through our home, memories through these bellies, tipsy straight whiskeys through honeys and sons, time can blindfold my ribcage, de-language my tongue, for all these floorboards eventually bust open, breathe, swallow, forget me, from the attic to the pantry, when the record skips the record skips, the fumbling lips, the draperies billow with ghosts, I will still echolocate your heartbeat in these walls.

In these walls the stairwell swells with silver song. My fingers tap along the railing with the spirit of Gregory Hines as pareidolias shine through the panes. I plastered on the ceiling precisely how that easy lemon in the sky looked the night I first met you, encouraging me to catch you, how it haloed over your roof as if it was proof this is our promised land where our holy-holies and heathens can come together in a marriage of ritual seducing tradition without judgment. Let the good feelings, the no regrets, the rebuilt self-esteems relax, breathe,

swallow…

These walls contain moments. My moments:

Like that time I was so high my face felt like a mush of something between oatmeal and butter, how it poured into the quark-speckled bowl of the cosmos, filling in cracks with quantum abstracts, the world ceasing to stutter…Like the day I helped my roommate's cat put a mouse's life to an end, only to realize all I had done was kill the cat's best friend, she spent a week lamenting in the basement, never purred for me again and I can't say I blame her so…Like when I learned Jimmy Eat World is not Earthworm Jim and Jack said, *The worms eat away but don't worry watch the wind! Yeah, the worms eat away but don't worry watch the wind!* I awoke, I arose, this drowsy sleeper from the night's Plutonian shore. Skip the ol' Medora, skip the roaring deep, lay down the waltzed Matilda, I know the lost Lenore is a home I'll never be for you are with me in these walls.

Life and death are in these walls. The laughing baby on a blue towel, how it melts into the mattress. Our bedroom gives birth to generations as children in the clawfoot tub slide on their soapy suds into a valley of imaginary water. Now the artist dreams with us. But the mailbox keeps half its promises. Each letter keeps asking, *What is power?* So an empty mother keeps tossing them into the pink and yellow room with the ever-made bed of petrified dolls and teddy bears, she knows this is where the answer lies, she knows power is when the last act on this Earth of a 5-year-old girl dying of cancer was to simply draw a butterfly taking flight from a flower. That is power. And you can still hear her fluttering in these walls.

Sometimes I ramble these darkened halls wondering what it is to be my grandfather, with antique eyes, elder mind washed out by the sunlight, colors so bright the glint found them too precious to let go. I once spotted Grandpa's legs in the fireplace, in a game of hide-and-go-seek where my sister and I would compete against the naps that stalled our adventures, making us drunk with dreams we still don't understand. We'd let Grandpa fall asleep then sneak back to our jungle gym fantasies juiced up on the sandwiched eggs he'd let us eat for a treat while watching the *Price is Right,* where I would sit puzzling over Plinko chips and how my grandfather wound up in the fireplace when I swear I saw him go down into the cellar. I think about his journey through the crawl space, how every partition I've ever put my ear to since traces the memory of him, and that memory now climbs through these walls

just as I am climbing with you.

Your furnace toasts these humbled toes, the vents are hoarding lost receipts, with pillows poised on our teeth we brush beliefs with tiny feathers to rustle forth some intricate heirloom that swings from the ceiling lamps, sings obscene nursery chants, enjoys getting fatter and fatter, then poses naked on a cake platter until it's frozen in a portrait on the family wall, prompting us to have faith in our sofa cushion forts, to put brand-new skate marks on our linoleum floor, to let the dining room dance free-form, dizzy dishes spooling spaghetti around the sconces, those China-chipped nuances our hearts would like to know, they zip arias across the table, there is mezzo in our matzo, stomachs listen to pasta operas just as I am listening for you

because your voice is in these walls

so I will tear them down and take them with me, my fingers puncturing drywall, perforating whatever circumference my arms can reach, like a wild creature I'll run through this house collecting ripped-out slabs for the pile, wallpapered continents stacked like flapjacks, snapping off in lightning cracks as I burrow through these rooms where you are bound, trying to save you, before the primordial sledge hammer condemns every piece of you to the ground, I want your splinters in my skin, your gypsum powder in my hair, want to carry it all with the nectar intact, this honey bee to a new hive, pollinating the roots, stashing fruit inside, crumbling continents between mortar and pestle, the aroma from the dust being breathed in, swallowed, stinging me, both causing and curing homesickness at the same time, I'll mix the wetness from my eyes with dirt and clay, discover in it new walls, with a new living room, new kitchen, second floor, clothes, sheets, bookshelves, hot chocolates, and heartbeats, let me run through those rooms bellowing my existence, my jaw is hungry for joy, my fists for any future, I live for soft lips and laughter, for severe thunderstorm warnings and the puddles left after, for the brave words that survive seasons of lonely mutters, for stuttering brothers with shy affections, for the women who promise to love them, for the bakie wakie muncheons, the wheat penny collections, and the stranger-than-fictions embedded in me, I will share them with you, explore them through and through, wear out my feet walking room to room secure within your structure, searching for treasure maps and wisdom, approaching each night like it's the first light of day, we hide and we go seek, I love how getting lost in you is the same as finding my way!

…The vinyl smells like peppermint. Let the record play.

I curl up to the newel post, puff unswept cat hair down a flight of stairs. It drifts away like delicate years into the foyer's vast embrace—I carry it all with me in a snow globe, never a day goes by I don't look inside and see my stay here was exactly the length it was supposed to be.

In these walls: Home.

time is an illusion

love is not

Punky's Funeral Pyre: Grandpa Reid

My grandpa used to put the pontoon top down
on thirty acres of land he simply called The River.
He was a farm boy WWII vet who worked for Guernsey Dairy
back when milkmen were still in high demand.

We used to get chocolate chip cookies from Kwik Trip, roast beef
sandwiches from Hardee's, he would tell me stories of silver fishing line
threading its way through marble currents a-swirl like a sawmill
and he'd call me *Jimmy Jim James, The Meanest Kid In All The Land!*

…But the boat dock soon gives up all its hitch knots, pontoon
        drifting like a downriver song.

Bury this sawblade, his wedding suit no longer fits right.
Scatter the sawdust, the landscape no longer dreams.

   My grandpa no longer knows my name.

He searches in the night for items he never lost
trying to conjure up a wife he barely remembers. She hides
in his wallet, in the rolltop desk, beneath the cushions of the davenport,
        calling his name. He searches for her
until the neighborhood drips out no more angels.
He searches for her until all the ice cream is gone.
He searches for her until ghost-shaken hands guide him back to bed.
He searches for her until his war medals are found.
He searches for her until he falls through the diamond earth, becomes infinity,
awakes in church portraits and VHS tapes, where I hear him calling my name,
where I hear all of them calling my name through family reunions
        these tablefuls of dead relatives, they say

                The daylight dims
                The cornfields scheme
                The worms will soon be biting

Then their voices go like exploding gravestones.
        My memories are on fire.

PUNKY'S FUNERAL PYRE

On the Logic of Love

some will say Love is irrational
Love is warlike, Love is mad

but this is Love misidentified

this is the name of Love falling victim
to confused reckless individuals
trying to justify their own mad & irrational ways

       in truth
Love is the highest form of logic

only when we recognize this, discover it in our blood
will the gaping wounds between emotion & reason
      be bridged & mended

only then will humanity walk in step once again
with the nature from which she comes

it's not: all is fair in Love & war

      it's:
war is rendered meaningless in the presence of Love

she is a flower in the fabric of space-time
handstitched and folded with dimension

Sweet Dream Ash

…a midnight purple powder that I breathe.

She stands on a flat stone, stares out to sea,
notes of Liebestraum No. 3 splashing her feet.
        The sky welcomes her.
Sliding its summer bright blue into night
it settles in and listens to her songs.
Songs about angels that betray our heavens
about smiles that bust at the heart
about a candle that burns alone in the dark
while a thousand loving hands can be seen
reaching at the light's edge but are forever out of reach
and once upon a time she built a fire on the beach
but it fell apart into sweet dream ash: a fragrance
        in the air we breathe.

She tells the sky about why she laughs, about the thousand fragments of
piano keys embedded in her chest, tickling her soul, about the cold punch lines
of sociopaths plunged into her back, about the side-splitting wrath of the angel
that betrayed her heaven, of the smile that busted her heart, and all she ever
hoped was for a love to lead her through the dark, lead each other to the fire,
rub lips with the sisterhood of psalms and flowers, crying vows with blissful
anarchy until this universe explodes into the next—so she had peeled
her guts from her belly, mind from her skull, fear from her heart, took all
those tissue-torn pieces she used for trusting, shoved their raw beauty forward
and this creature *raped her trust* with secret lovers kept beneath its wings,
with relationships on puppet strings and two-way mirrored truths destroying
this love, this dream. This love. Dream. Love! Dream! She

        LAUGHS!
Her hopes buckle, she begins to fall apart!
That's when the sky cries, the wind swoops in,
kisses her forehead and says, "Whoooooooooooosssssssssssssssssssssss
sssssssssssssssssssssssssssssssssssssssssssssssssSSSSSSSSSSSSSSSSSSSSSSSSSS
SSSSSSSSSSSHHHHHHHhhhhhhhhhhhh-sssssssshhhhhh-shhh-shh-shh…!"

        She turns.

Still standing on that flat stone, she turns
and stares at me, the language of Liszt licking her feet.

  I tell her we can build fires together

that I don't have wings but baby we can still fly
and when we fall we can fall into each other.
We can waltz, two-step, jitterbug, twist again like awesome fools
then kiss against the moon because darling
I have nothing I wish to sell, I will give this love to you.

    She smiles
and walks with me across the sand and stones
back to our little camp on the beach
where I pluck out those punch lines and piano keys
use them as tinder, make some heat
then we lie down lacing our fingers together until we have a solid grip
and in her ear I whisper, *Sweet dreams, Ash!*

And the waves yawn along the shore their faint song:
        ah-ahhh ahhh ahhh
        ah-ahhh ah-ahhh ah-ahhhhh-ah...

And when the sky looks down it sees two hands holding in the light
as our fire turns to embers, as embers melt into purple powder
which the wind then blows upon us, covering our skin,

    blessing us with a sweet dream.

No Attic in the Attic

A new husband unloads knickknacks.

His wife calls from above: *Help me, sweetie!*
This attic's a labyrinth! I can't find my way round at all!

So he leaves his boxes, climbs two stairwells
then finally reaches—the cellar.

Dizzy as an astronaut, ill-at-ease with reality's glitch
he yells a high-pitched, *Coming!*

Galloping the first and second floors
he punches the last steps to—yet again, the cellar!

He frantically loops for hours. Then days.
Fetches docs, scientists. None have an answer.

Years elapse. Her voice no longer casts
yet faithful husband clambers upward.

And this poor man will ascend the steps until his stomping rots away.
For there's no attic in the attic, just a hollow haunt of love.

In a Wish

in a wish   you dip your thoughts in
a baffling brook of golden consciousness
where truth lies like a shifty tide
washing upon the shore a heavy billow of light
wherein you find something missing but not fully
                              missed
in a wish   you close your eyes and he is still
the outline memory keeps in its sketches, still and silent
is his open heart, so you press the image
with your own pulse, remembering rhythms
no longer distinguishable in their validity
                    only
in a wish   the ghostly vapor, the phantom physicality
like so much muscle memory teasing itself in the mirror
after a moment he is gone with the candle's fog
still there is kept a small happiness that with you
                    only can exist

former lovers
fill the corridors of the maze
with bittersweet dittos

Poison on Your Honeymoon

she ate a monarch butterfly

   crunchy cracker jack

salty sweet like Beethoven

like elderberry wine ripening

like an old busted lock with a shiny brass key

it fits   but only

      for now

Separated

and it's been twenty years
and his kids have all moved out
and not once has he heard from her since
          still
his midnight façade is plagued by two quivering ghosts of her
still there is a stubborn song that carries her through him
like a lights-out child brought home to bedtime's ringing
like an old man suckling Death's teat raw

      and Death says,
    I am all you've left undone

The Old Woman in the Attic

Before I say goodbye, you ought to know:
the torment from dead kisses fades away.
With this I'll say goodbye, with this I'll go.

If young flames could return to candle's glow,
if hearts could pour again, you'd hear them say,
  Before I say goodbye, you ought to know.

The cost of true love's joy will never show.
When sorrow weeps it keeps the light from day.
With this I'll say goodbye, with this I'll go.

Beneath your bosom, oceans ebb and flow
while flesh and bone must hold my soul at bay.
Before I say goodbye, you ought to know

the missteps in this world might haunt us so,
through rhapsodies we'll dance a true ballet.
With this I'll say goodbye, with this I'll go.

When shrouded ravens come to count our crows
may unsaid love be not among their prey.
Before this last farewell, will your heart know?

  With this I say goodbye. With this I go.

Dark Beauty Blooming

in the end Death arrived
not as a monster, not as a bully
not a cruel or cold blank nightmare

    in love it arrived
revealing itself a perfect gentleness
who greeted them honest sympathies
through several gestures of wisdom

who told them
        I promise to take the greatest care with her
        protect her from fear, grief, and suffering
        to never leave her side
        as she drifts the realm of dreams
        you helped her build

who then bid them farewell
turned with her toward the sunset
dark beauty blooming, they pushed ahead
a sweet and forward light

Ghost Rose Green

  ghost   rose   green

scar let my face once healed

dead music this is sour

sweet sour ball candy greens

ghost both a have-to and a must

but a rose gone

gone milk dew

gone silkweed

gone green lily pads of busty bold beauty

sweet eat sweet scar

no ghost here scar

eat oh sweet ghost rose green

oh sweet scar

my green face

once healed

she made a jukebox out of him
what with how his thoughts
kept flipping records of her

Punky's Funeral Pyre: Kitten

I met Kitten near the woodland's edge, on the hilltop-side of adventure
where a stroll and a laugh once weaved us through the tree line
    where we dared to dream in the other's eye.

But star-crossed paths get scorched by young love's temper.
Our garden got drenched in pesticides, reducing rose petals to devils or saints.

    Now we no longer fit right.

She no longer remembers the sweet laziness we held between us:
the way my lips prayed to hers, each tiny wish I slipped behind her ears,
the fingers that swam through our hair, how she *swayed* on her toes to kiss me.

She no longer remembers when that gun went off in the apartment below
and holy shit I wouldn't be anything less than her bomb shelter that night
the night we first made love she no longer remembers how when she slept
I held her in tears of joy and fear, begging my flesh, my bones, my faith
to be enough to someday save her…On second thought, that last one is
something she'll just never know, like my visions of a firstborn daughter
with the same green eyes, the same determined chin. How I loved her
in a way both rare and true…She no longer remembers the sweet.

    But I remember all of her.

I remember every prayer tucked inside a rice paper lantern, fierce as fate,
glowing like a pointillist's painting of a hundred billion neurons suspended
in my cranium. Our lives breathe in the space between, we must step back
to see the synapses are balloon strings, they tremble as they wait to be released.

    Every tale of *you & me*

        made you

        made me.

Hands tremble as they wait to be released.

    Our memories are on fire.

Arrow's Precision

A steady *whoosh!*—an arrow flew.
Damn the cherub with the powder-soft cheeks.

I scoped the feathered missle's path, began to panic,
assuming a fool's expertise about the nature of heartstrings.

As the impact approached I
cringed in cowardice, shrieking.

The arrowhead's precision struck the twisted ropes
that tied me to the bricks and cinderblocks

      setting everything free

All the note said to the empty house:

Happier now.

The Pressed Flower

It's at the Piggly Wiggly in our hometown where we appear
in aisle 5 with the coffee beans and boxes of tea
like one pleasant surprise placed face-to-face with another.

In your eye lies a remaining whisper
threading back through all the days now past
to a beginning long outgrown, feet

still dancing faint flutters to severed songs
of summertime skipping beats across the waves,
and always will it be said how it's been too long.

We can easily see how those in-between years
hold countless days of discovery, of loss,
of small worlds unfolded and reaching back
upon themselves in breathless spectacles of story
that shine light on the backs of our throats
but fall ever short of our tongues

for a knowing glance at the teething miracle in your shopping cart
brings back a flood of silent respect

and even though we could talk
until the last letter of the last story
radiates from our well-worn lips, we allow ourselves
only time enough to hug, to wish the best,
to say, *Hey, go enjoy the rest of your day!*

TRAVELING CHARACTER ACTORS

Come crystal dust inside my mind
Come kings and queens who wish to play
We'll build new worlds and in them find
All we thought lost in yesterday

Drifter in Rome

I am made of rags and I have a hole in my pocket.

...Did I say pocket?

I meant the palm of my hand. It's where I feed broken
piano keys, a library of melodies and dissonant chords.

How can I shake these disrupted lifelines?
    I don't trust the letter *m, m*other
    I don't trust the letter *f, p*ops
with their serifs, their paraffin lips liquefying
while a rooster croons from its pulpit about the profits of man.

In my other hand there is a pocket filled with true love
for a stranger, with praises expressed in native tongues

with berries, chocolate chews, living stories
and a complete collection of mended holes.

The Driftless

I had been walking along a gravel path for several hours
without meeting any crossroads, cars, or people

eventually there came a break between the trees and tall grass, where a field
opened up, guiding my eyes toward an old well dotted in the distance

having grown ever so thirsty I dragged my feet across the field
and found a tin cup of icy clear beverage waiting for me

I downed the drink and felt refreshed enough
but my body was still a heavy bundle of exhaustion

so the evening sun convinced me to stay and rest
while it forged on ahead, to scout out tomorrow's terrain

I sat leaning against the old well, my back relaxing into the rock slab
with surprising ease, and before I knew it the grass was sprouting through
my legs, wrapping around them in a thick coat, warming my bones

and as night fell more and more into its deep dive
my head turned more solidly into a wooden bucket rotted
and stamped with the jagged grin of a brown jack-o'-lantern

a frozen expression fixed atop the neck of a slouching scarecrow
all my candles reignited, all my dreams cast in stone

Through Thick Fog

the fire escapes and busted drains are dripping down on the invisible man
you can see his wayward smile when the wind blows east

she speaks on behalf of the broken boys, teaches the window frame how
to hold wishes, she believes her European dream is coming back someday

lick the envelopes, pass the mashes, none of those instant grits for the holiday
I twist the rabbit ears on the console just to hear them say

> *mama o mama, I'll be a headline tomorrow*
> *they dip the quill tip in my blood to get the black print on their page*

> *father o father, forgive these hypochrists among us*
> *for they know not what they do or the ungodly price that's paid*

an exorcist damned and dizzy, fed up with sham mythology,
serves the girl a dash of sticky hash, dancing shadows turn to stone

hot air balloon filled my mind then fled: it was a blue dream, it was
a train wreck, now a silver shell goes swimming over sunny San Rafael

Cosmo Kal moves to Pocatello, her face all pentimento
she cannot decide on a baby inside or another scheme to sell

> *ha'lujah! ha'lujah!, open says I!, abracablam!*
> *here's the last coin in my pocket for the gold in which you stand*

> *believer believer, ignorance is broad not bliss, speak with reason*
> *not your fists—love becomes a fairy tale in your esoteric hell*

dungarees and a macaroon sneak into the honeymoon suite
where time flies like a banana cream pie for fifty-odd years

grab universe man by his tickity nose, he loves season two
of the Twilight Zone, now he's watching the Monsoon Man,
the Taking of Pelham, High Noon Saloon, and the Sting

Jayhawk and Vanya eat at Gobble & Squat with Mister Potter and his jester, Copperpot—I think they've waited for you, Neil, from behind the trees

> *together my lover we be a happy piece of furniture, a script by an aging typewriter, white chocolate in a soap dish, tumbling like a hologram down a well*

> *dharma o dharma, sing your songs of karma like you've never seen a soul before, this ghost train haze might get us home, don't go riding yet another throwaway line*

> *the invisible man goes walking tonight*

Like Any Other Rainy Day

scat-man phrases puddle in unhinged minds slivered open
by electric orange peels and Pop Rocks chocolatiered into
free samples from Seroogy's melting over Norah Jones's voice

wet washboard winds snatch at see-thru umbrellas
            streets shine like glass
faerie tales curl like kittens on windowsills while
cobweb candle wicks sleep in shadowed libraries

                  the city:
            a watered crisp garden

Downpour

flash-frozen puddles ripple into existence
like glass oracles floating above snow

chance bends at their mercy
weaving whirlwinds into wrinkles

when streetlights illuminate
they burn like pools of gold

Blind as Stone

I mocked a man blind as stone
while waiting at a corner.

My mimicked cane-thrusts threw my balance
off the curb, at a passing bus.

The man quickly reached out,
pulled me toward him,

and gave me back my eyes.

Bad Actors

Compact smeared mirrors
snap shut. Characters
pretend to listen. Off-
stage drama is a smog
stuck inside lungs speaking
bright words to draw in
starlight—want to be
yet are not to be.

Look! Résumés written on golden paper!
Look how they namedrop celebrities!

Keep looking—up here! Away from
    shallow artwork
    slipshod craft
    drip-drop dialects.
These are not artists. No,

these are bad actors

whose gilded personalities
make bad theatre more real than
their martini confessions. Fiction
being published as non-fiction.

My Brother

My brother's buying some late-night drive-thru tacos
finds an empty parking lot, takes two bites
and starts to choke on his tears, throws
the meat and shells onto cracked concrete.

He cries confined in his self-made solitude
because he's lost and fat and feels too old at thirty
to love himself enough to let his parents find love in him.

As he tries to catch his breath, his heavy chest trembling,
despair's miserable voice forces its way up his throat:
    escaping as shrill staccato wails
    tapering in leaky muffled defeat
never reaching the edges of the parking lot.

He wants to forget these goddamn gaslights, overused
check cards, midnight binges, trashy apartments.
Forget it all and let a father's hug, a mother's kiss
make him innocent again.
                Instead,
the darkness leaves him hungry with no appetite
with only his car engine coughing in cold air
    and a broken taco to believe in.

Impostor

Monty Python glows on my television screen. Surround sound
vibrates the whiskey bottle erect on the see-thru surface of glass.

Pizza grease and flattened soda punctuate the air as a suburban living room
fades into a summer night. Lampshades reflect their reversed reality over
twilight-cool windowpanes. Street-lit eyes peer down into private quarters,
where a dormant phone stands as immobile structures do
when a lack of events overrules your weekend into isolation.

Droning *bohms!* from a mantelpiece clock record the hour-within-minute
increments crunching their way down a dwindling chip bag and aching
stomach, forming the only hourglass I need.

When morning returns and Earth again acknowledges existence, I shower,
grab a book, then meet my friends at the opera house to portray all I'm not.

Good Actors

sound editors, film editors
will spend hours tweaking
a wave of noise or light,
lovingly whittle their way
toward dreamed masterpieces
shared by musicians who break
through beastful chord switches,
the painter who is going to *goddamn it*
paint a realistic-fucking-looking hand
if it fucking kills me—these engineers
with well-polished processes funneling
like water into the wide-open groove of catharsis
must the actor likewise be such, understanding
the frequencies within a character, the worlds within a word,
the art of it no longer a passing nightly ship, but now—and quite rightly so—
      a lifelong partner

Actor in Empty Space

I don't know why
lights focus at the angles they do
why the gels were blue and not pink
or why we can't break through the fourth wall
without one of us being something untrue

I don't know why
the director is unseen
why the actor stands alone in front of the screen
or why the screen is both
the wide-open sky and a wall

I don't know why
two truths can't combine
why one show can't play until another's curtain closes
or why we can't hear heroes
until the heroes are gone

HINDSIGHT
&
OTHER VISIONS

Even when I say,
Yes, sweet self, escape for now,
space and time say,

No.

Perseverance

near the center of the world
deep within a cave
buried in a rubble-filled room
hidden inside a giant sealed safe
frozen in a concrete coffin
locked inside an ancient chest
stashed within a chain-mail bag
wrapped in golden silk
being what it can be
is a sign that reads:

DON'T GIVE UP!

Hindsight

Hindsight is not a time machine. She can't pendulate
back and forth, just BACK, RESET, and BACK again.

      I built her bones inside my garage.
Forking through scrap-metal salads, I clicked and cranked together
triangle after triangle until they formed a skeletal globe, extended
struts and joints from its crust to the junkyard car seat at its core,
installed a central nervous system of magnets, lights, electricity.
By the time I finished it looked like a particle collider had been
      swallowed up by a Hoberman sphere.

Back then I kept in my breast pocket a folded-up piece of paper
with different months and cities written on it, months like

    November 2008 – Mumbai, India
    April 1995 – Oklahoma City, Oklahoma
    May 1974 – Ma'alot, Israel
    November 2015 – Paris, France
    September 2001 – New York City, New York

    …To name a few.

Sitting in that junkyard car seat, I balanced the dials on my arm rest,
      tugged my seat belt, flicked the switch.

The lights darted inward. Positive magnets chased them
in hot pursuit, toward Hindsight's negative core. The frame
collapsed upon itself. When the light reached the center
with nowhere else to run, the magnets caught up, bumping
light off continuum's cliff. The framing followed.
      My ship and I winked away.

The little silver ball fell back with yester-daze
down ruffled trails of cosmic fabric
rolling to a rest on an empire shiny and new
where a dozen shadows once crashed into the daylight
toppled people over, left rubbles of stolen dreams.

I arrived as the shadows were shaping
raced to warn the kings, philosophers, children, to tell them about the bomb
but they looked at me a fool, squeezed their egocentric blankies
        said, *Goddamn and kingdom come!*

    I hastened to their parents—who knew!
Who saw this falling nightmare, this oncoming curse!
I begged and I begged but they looked at me with pity
        while stating, *Nothing can be done.*

So I infiltrated the darkness to curb the shadows alone,
stomping on combat boots and a rebel gun…Except
trying to fend off darkness is like trying to capture light:
hands struggle for a grip yet hold nothing in the end.
Where I thought I brought newfangled variables, I found myself
within the equation, hidden behind unknowns. For every shot
I meant to block was another innocent couple dead on their loveseat,
stray bullet hole staring at them through their living room wall.

As gloom pushed heavy on the quivering city, I dragged myself back
into my spheroid ship, RESET Hindsight's bearings, switched away.

Restored inside my garage, I slumped over the seat belt, waiting
for heart and stomach to join the team. A neighborhood breeze
escaped from the street, through a window, caressing freshness
on my wet and furrowed brow. My ship said,

    The universe can't take back what it has already spoken.

Nodding, I jettisoned my list of dates where history seemed too cruel
and vowed to only fuss with the ever here and now.

Now I ride, a tourist, through that scope of god-like memories.
And she graciously takes me. Not a time machine.

        Just Hindsight.

meditate and undress pain
like rose petals sizzling off the bone

The Medically Induced Coma (In a Perfect World)

A man stood beside a warm hospital bed
Watching his son die one piece at a time.

He still might survive, the kind doctor said.
There's one more solution we haven't tried.
But the plan is quite dangerous, your boy is in much pain,
When he goes to sleep now you might not see him again.
So stand by his side, let him see your face,
Say something soothing as his rhythm is slowing.

And the man told the doctor, *What on Earth do I say?*
Do I tell him Goodbye? Or it will be Okay?
Do I tell him these things happen while the gods are away?
This is not right, Doc, this is not supposed to be.
Children are meant to stay, parents are meant to leave.
This should be me, Doc—should be me.

And the kind doctor said: *In a perfect world.*

The son then stirred, spoke through feeble lips:
Father, don't bother with the black pits of sorrow,
Don't busy your heart with perfect scripts,
Don't dwell on before or if I'll be here tomorrow.
Just say I Love You. And let the words thrive.
'Cause whether you've been here awhile or you've only just arrived,

   I Love You is its own place.

Doesn't matter if you're coming or going.

Möbius

I will be am who was before
the am who is, who was no more
who will be then when then is now
till now is not quite here somehow

Give me a half-twist—this band, this width
this single boundary reaching forward for that asymptote.

My eyes are pillars of books that out-stack those alpine heavens
stories flapping open-faced along this strip of verity
of dreams alive and giant, the way your dreams use to be.
But now you fade from our *mise-en-scène*, afraid
of being sliced out from that colossal film reel
and left behind on the cutting room floor.

When I was a boy I once asked if you believed in a god.
You said gods perhaps only exist when you are thinking about them
and probably not even then. I asked if you believed the world as myth.
You said faith is a moment and this moment is missing.

      This moment is missing.

Or maybe faith, as a concept, has been turned inside-out,
worn on the wrong hand…Do I believe in a god?
      I believe in light, I believe in darkness.
      I believe in all the love found in-between.
I believe the calmness that keeps old age from fearing death's apparent horizon
is in knowing how this line, if continued, will meet its starting point again—
      a persistence of perception.

One day you announce to us: *Family and friends,*
      I have cancer, I am not dying.
      I have cancer, I am not dying.
And that day you aren't. Neither are you the day after.

But as each new terror is detected the calendar grows heavy with emptiness
      our home three times its gravity

where I must sit witnessing this anti-miracle of breath to bones. I read books
describing how we one day translate back to our projection point
not understanding the moral of this story. My burdens get the best of me
like the anxious shepherd with his out of control flock, sheep pulling woes
over our eyes as we behold you, your future history slipping away,
struggles cementing into permanence, bankrupting unfinished business,
slowly ripping you from us with no regard to quality, until one day
I lose faith in the middle of a cold shower, drowning in
every innocent tear I hear suffer, and wish a silent wish
for you to die, betraying the bonds of brotherhood, of friendship,
the spirit of survival—forgive me, please, my friend,
                    forgive me, please!

You woke from your soon-to-be-eternal sleep to tell us two things:
          1. Be sure to spread happiness, move time forward.
          2. I love each and every one of you.

The reel uncoils itself from the projector, lies flat,
then is raised from the floor in ceremony.
It's given a half-twist and joined start to finish.

          Is this not what now is?
          Is this not what faith is?
          Is this what I am?

               I will be am who was before
               the am who was, who is no more
               who will be then when then is now
               yet now is not quite here somehow

74

Such Sweet Sorrow

when are you leaving, soulmate?
        kiss the tear-stained cheek
        cradle the neck like holy grail
when will you go?
        late light, the frightening feeling
        as two minds savor the last memory meal
soulmate?
        new egg crackling loud as the lightning-struck mountain
        recalls country drives through handheld days of silent love
are you?
        yester-laughing calm sheet rising chest—kiss me
        stay until all this richness
                       gone?

they asked:
what is it like to lose a friend?

she replied:
it is to visit the grey-lit land
that lies opposite the joy of discovery

Supernova's Aftermath

every nebula bows to the black hole

the whirlpool reaches out, clutches
all those trinkets of the universe
close to its chest, compresses them
into a single moment without worry,
        without time

        it's not evil
it merely wants to maintain melting visions
the way all observers do, hide and
preserve them with eternal revelry,
cherish them for their absoluteness
like Hawking's theory of everything

Meteor

drips stardust
puncturing skies with ferocious hope

whispers
       meet me
    at the other end
    of the universe

twinkle twinkle
little dreams

explode

Postmortem

i
He could look back.
He could stand at the beginning and look forward.
He could watch diners pass around ceramic cups of black coffee, could watch
locks of hair from one person's head find another person's shoulder. He
could see the mosaic emotions from every world he had ever met,
the tears never drying, the laughter never growing old.

ii
He enjoyed looking at it all from the side
where music blooms into stalagmite sounds musicians once heard
dripping from above, where angry war slithers along with its severed head,
where an old theatre emerges like a majestic whale resurfacing to breathe,
where every life is the eye of an hourglass, and those sweet
permanent streaks of comet tails burst with all the complexity
the universe leaves behind while passing through a single soul.

iii
His thoughts run a straight line through curved space.
The cones in his eyes wrap infinity arcs around his mind,
sweeping nows and thens like a hyperspatial pendulum.
He once heard the chatter of innocent starlight, it blipped out
blueprints for time machines that he wrote down and posted on the fridge.
Four time machine settings become obvious to old souls and young minds:
    Past, Present, Future, and Meanwhile.

iv
The concrete world began to spin, condensate,
flow in and out of itself in thick clouds of remembrance.
He went not to his last moments but to his favorite moments:
He is laughing at a funeral. He is reading his first science fiction.
He is a midnight vow on his honeymoon too sacred for the ears of witnesses.
He is brotherly love, sharing a booth with joyous friends, passing
good stories over damn good food. He is in rehearsal, directing.
He is a genius child with eyes of roaring sapphire, new thoughts
appear to him like strange ghosts escaping the space-time vortex,
they whisper random details of a happy life. He is smiling.

v

The only noise is streetlight. He considers all these things:
the laughter audible, the nows even closer than before.
He is in a warm bed, his book bookmarked.
A shooting star flickers briefly in the inked sky.
The shell falls to Earth. The light shines.
Onward.

absorb   life

               time

               emit

               time   love

KALACHAKRA
(PART 2)

which is me
which is you
as we wish-dream
through this who?

Into Existence

a skull blossom
        blending light and thought

inspiration caught
        in the cranium

blooms in a blink
        like a brand-new universe, it is

beyond your own flesh
        your cradled electric heart

pumping creation
        into a complex system of love

where infinity's eyes
        emit stardust
pollinate reality with winged dreams

until butterflies chase bullets
        and eventually surpass them

A River of Consciousness

     tell the prophet to come

skyscrapers burn as children fall into
evanescent desire, deeply embedded
deeply embedded so long as I keep writing

so long to you as you journey through
thousands of years and worlds of time

complacency cast its stone, withered to the ocean
while man evolved into religion, while religion
built its stars, demanding the rights to heaven

     but there is none

only empty hope believing in living after
we're supposed to be done living, painting
wrangling rippling images on a canvas
projected to all corners of Earth

head me home with shoes to remove
with bed as a keepsake for nocturnal indulgence
but let me roam freely through my dreams
let me save, let me love, let me perish
in the dreams that I've foreseen for dreaming

     perception is a fingerprint

Underground Mansions

another night of this burnt-out sleep
filled with scenes from your living grave
where those hollow drowned heartaches creep
already lost but you're still trying to save them
still trying to save at least one
                              from this stone-slab street
boulevard of a dead friend's gaze
they rummage nightmares for their heartbeat heat
speaking love like a shifting maze
shifting faces in the tombs of your doubt
you guess at riddles so fragile they shake
                              but can you guess
the trespasser's name, this multiverse chain
molding valleys in your burnt-out sleep
                    where you wake and you wake and you wake
on a bed of broken riddled bo-peeps
speaking truth in its quiet haze
                    you wake and you wake and you wake
and all this truth is a quiet
this truth is so quiet you shake
                    then you wake and you wake and you wake
                    oh you wake and you wake and you wake
        to this burnt-out dream
basement's end brings a mansioned-out cave
filled with stories you will never complete
fiendish figures dwell in darkish hallways
ever-lurking at the heels of your feet
they stole your father, they stole your true-love voice
they stole your breadcrumbs, you can never go back
cliffs and canyons plunge through the velvet noise
to a leap of fate where dares of courage will be asked
        all-knowing eyes
            burst through
                this verse to you
                    and ask
                are you awake? you awake? you awake?
you seek the ballroom where drifters mend their blues

awaiting news from a faraway hope
                          you awake? you awake? you awake?
there are no ceilings here just chandeliers and moons
floating like beasts through a sea-bottom throat
and all this meaning is mindless, this meaning so mindless it breaks you
                          awake and awake and awake
do you walk through your burnt-out sleep
asking every new face,
                you awake?
another night of this stone-dead speak
spitting blood into your far-out haze
you fend off murder on an endless repeat
plotlines bending through each unpleasant phase
those hidden chambers in your language dissolve
we've no more world left for us to embrace
arm-hair spiders in the evening evolve
and now they say that you can't shake

        some little problem you keep meaning to solve

                          when you wake and you wake and you wake
your brain keeps schticking with stooges
like holes tied together with string
like bonebird flying on a loose-bolt wing
                          you wake and you wake and you wake
there's no more time left for you to escape
                          when you wake and you wake and you wake
and you're still searching for endings
still searching for an end to this rain
you hear the answer
                barely whisper
                      your name
                then you wake and you wake and you wake
                oh yes you wake and you wake and you wake
we see you fall through this burnt-out dream
        asking faces if ever you'll wake

When You Wake

you hear distant rumors about what it will be like
to go to sleep and never wake up

about a time when all vibrations cash in their casino chips, take
      the red-eye home
when the biggest number is again smaller than the smallest number
when your mind is a wilting flower and an hour yet pending
returns you to the realm that fed you into birth

you hear these things happening someday

but today you breathe fire and music as if fire and music, like yourself, were
somehow separate from this collapsing dream of time trying to remember light

you have always been light
light is the reality beneath the dream

as you are breath, you are the nothingness
a photon knows not its own existence

so why fear the wilted flower?

if the color has gone pallid
the leaves too brittle to touch
then cheer the fragrance

it is still so incredible and lovely

Comforting Death

I found Death in fetus pose, sickle thrown aside,
asked which grieving flavor brought forth its wailing sighs.

         Death replied:
Love can't see my face inside my ghastly world.
And I can't—no, I'm too scared—I just can't remove my robes.

I looked at Death and told it straight, *No, that is not true.*
Just as Death is all around, I assure you: Love is too.

You and Love are intertwined—one fabric from one thread.
This side first claimed, I am alive. *The other*, I am dead.

Since those utmost declarations there has never been a doubt
that Love is Death and Death is Love, forever inside-out.

Death then stood, attempted a grin—more honest tries I'll never know—
then sighed once more and spoke to me, *You know it's time to go?*

I nodded comprehension. And slipped its arm in mine.
And focused on the infinite peace in that forest without time.

It whispered along the journey, like a soothing midnight tune, saying
Thank you, for now I remember that—like Love—Death lives too.

all of this
is a universe lit by ghost light

Brahman: Breaking Pralaya

at first it is silence

it is not darkness, it is not brightness—
it is a pregnant nothingness basking in
unmeasurable states of meditation

abstraction stirs self-awareness

silence gives birth to a small
humble vibrant song

The Silent Life

There's a high note
caught in your throat
and it's lodged, tangled up
in your weak nodes.

There's a cry with no sound
but I'm yelling a thousand times
as loud as you, as loud as
the open fields and sky.

I can hear a whispered song
in September grass, and life
does all its living as it dies.

We are all happening sideways at one time.

We the Firefly

Today: We are all unraveled, our lives pulled, exposing the accordion that blooms from the fragile bonds of our paper doll folds. We realize we are time travelers, lovers and killers, telepaths and dumb-luck dreamers. I am my father and my unborn son. I am the woman on the bus, the child in her arms, the driver cussing to himself as his pancreas flinches against each pothole.

And the universe reveals to us how we are the most unlikely of every fat truth, and the walls we climb daily are laden with false bricks that can be pushed in like a button, unlocking doors that lead to new space, but even there we get the feeling *We have been here before* over and over and over.

Somewhere in a run-down apartment there is an ancient prince. He's on his seventeenth life. He doesn't understand where he is, the noise in the street, or why these colosseums are dripping from his eyes.

There is a sparrow resting her wings. She's the embodiment of short and sweet and every day she's pretty sure that you and I and this whole damn world are something she dreamt up last night in her sleep.

We are loopers, rabbit hole divers, matrix upon matrix. There is the illusion we are each an individual essence when in truth we share one soul. It is a firefly caught between the canvas and the paint and it floats across this portrait of existence, filling each life as it does so. Meaning someday, somehow, you will be the person sitting next to you. Someway, somelife, you will see yourself from across the room.

Trust me, for I have been you. I have smiled all your smiles. Your hearts pump my blood. Our pulses are the waves, humanity the moon, I have been you. You are loners and regretters. Heavily you sit without a dream to hold your hand. I have seen you trying to crawl back through the rooms you have already walked through. As if you could rewind, cut, copy, paste, and create anew. As if that were some kind of miracle. But tall and glowing and tall and alive you have already walked through, I have seen you, you starlight, you midnight wanderers.

Don't worry about the phone calls from family you ignored, they have already forgiven you with hugs and pot roasts. Don't worry about the dead friends who visit your dreams again and again, they are not tormented or lost, it just means you love them so much more than the time they were given, for you are them and they are you. I have been you.

Do not fester in a heap of sour love gone wrong but rise above it so opportunity may find you. If you have hurts at the bottom of your heart, do not go looking at them through the bottoms of your drinks. Reach down, take them in your hands, crumble them to pieces and toss them up to the heavens that swallow everything yet say nothing. Because this life is a moving cliff and the day we were born was the day we let go, so unclench your fists, learn to make music with the air around your fingertips. The only moment is right-here/right-now and, right-here/right-now, you'll find every other moment. Be a moment. Be the wind that blows through the cemetery where children play. Be the relief in somebody's smile at the end of the day. Be these words, for they are no longer mine. Be soft lips for the springtime. Be boogie-woogie, jazz, and soul, be boogie-woogie, jazz, and soul. When something wrong is going down be the voice that yells, **NO!** *Be the Sun! Be the Moon! Be a cry for a cry and a truth for a truth!*

Today: Unravel with me. You are free. Me, I have been you. I have seen you without a dream to hold your hand—so hold my hand, and we the firefly will flow out a new path, resting now and then on the canvas, absorbing rich paint. For I have been you. And when I walk around this world, stare into your faces,
I know

you have been me too.

in the end
in the grand scheme
we are each
a cosmic daydream

musing

ACKNOWLEDGMENTS

Many thanks to the editors and staff of the following publications where these poems first appeared, sometimes in various forms:

The Binnacle, Machias, Maine; "Evergreen Fireworks"
Bramble Lit Magazine, Wisconsin; "Punky's Funeral Pyre: Grandpa Reid,"
      "*This Just In* – Local Ant News Bulletin (Broadcast Date: June 5, 2010)"
Fox Cry Review, Menasha, Wisconsin; "Bad Actors" & "The Silent Life"
Great: Poems of Resistance & Fortitude; "We the Firefly"
OPE!—A Pop-Up Anthology of Madison Writers & Artists, Madison,
      Wisconsin; "Chipper the (Dead) Chipmunk"
Penguin Review, Youngstown, Ohio; "Blind as Stone"
Poetry Hall, Chicago, Illinois; "Actor in Empty Space," "On the Logic of Love,"
      "Spring Makes True"
Teen Ink Magazine, Newton, Massachusetts; "A River of Consciousness"
Wisconsin People & Ideas, Madison, Wisconsin; "My Brother" & "No
      Attic in the Attic"

"In These Walls" contains the line "*the worms eat away but don't worry watch the wind*," which is from Jack Kerouac's song "Home I'll Never Be."

"Into Existence," "Meteor," "Music Lovers," "Postmortem," "Supernova's Aftermath," & "When You Wake" all first appeared in my chapbook, *Thoughts on Tonight*, published by Finishing Line Press in November of 2017.

"My Brother" & "No Attic in the Attic" received honorable mentions in the *Wisconsin People & Ideas* 2018 and 2019 Poetry Contests, respectively. "My Brother" also won the UW-Oshkosh Reeve Union Board 2010 Student Writing Contest in the categories of Poetry and Overall High Score.

"Say It Live" was first performed on WFRV's Local 5 Live on April 24, 2015, in Green Bay, Wisconsin, to help promote poetry events created and organized by Tori Grant Welhouse.

"Spare Room," "In These Walls," & "AMP" were written and first performed for HOME: A Group Art Exhibition, curated by Kyle J. Krueger on February 1 & 2, 2014, in Milwaukee, Wisconsin.

"Sweet Dream Ash" was first performed on February 28, 2013, as part of the poetry series, *Spitfire Thursdays at Gene's Supper Club*, hosted by Spitfire Shine in Milwaukee, Wisconsin, and is when I first entered the spoken word scene.

Poetry Hall is a Chinese-English bilingual journal where my poems "On the Logic of Love," "Spring Makes True," & "Actor in Empty Space" appeared in both languages, Chinese translations by Yang Zhongren (杨中仁译) & Feng Xiaoxia (冯晓霞译).

Extra thanks to Alaina Albaugh, Emily Bowles, Bruce Dethlefsen, James P. Roberts, the FLP staff, Gary Reid, & Ashley Beranek—without you, this book wouldn't be.

Spoken word poet NATHAN J. REID was born in Oshkosh, Wisconsin, where he grew up developing interests in theatre and writing. His first published poem was printed in *Teen Ink Magazine* in 2004, and his work has since appeared in the *Penguin Review, Fox Cry Review, Bramble Lit Magazine, Wisconsin People & Ideas, Poetry Hall, OPE!—A Pop-Up Anthology of Madison Writers & Artists, GREAT: Poems of Resistance & Fortitude* poetry anthology, and other publications. In September of 2019 he curated and emceed the *Constitutional Cabaret*, a poetry theatre event—he is also host of *The Reid Poetry Hour*, an annual radio show on WORT 89.9 FM. He serves on the boards of the Council for Wisconsin Writers, the Wisconsin Poet Laureate Commission, the Wisconsin Fellowship of Poets, and is the former senior editor for the *Wisconsin Review*. His first collection of poems, *Thoughts on Tonight*, was published in 2017 by Finishing Line Press.

Reid currently lives in Madison, Wisconsin with Swarmy and Calico Cici. In addition to artistic pursuits, he is an avid reader, occasional songwriter, amateur philosopher, and enthusiast of movies, quiz shows, travel, and chocolate.

Learn more about him and his most recent projects at nathanjreid.com.

www.ingramcontent.com/pod-product-compliance
Lightning Source LLC
Chambersburg PA
CBHW021149090426
42740CB00008B/1018